ANGEL CAKE'S
CUPCAKE BOOK

by Alison Saeger Panik

Scholastic Inc.

New York   Toronto   London   Auckland   Sydney   Mexico City   New Delhi   Hong Kong   Buenos Aires

ISBN 0-439-70311-5

Designer: Emily Muschinske
Illustrations: Lisa and Terry Workman
Photographs: Alison Saeger Panik

12 11 10 9 8 7 6 5 4 3 2 1   4 5 6 7 8 9/0
Printed in the U.S.A.
First Scholastic printing, November 2004

TABLE OF CONTENTS

Get Ready for a
SWEET ADVENTURE!

Hi, it's me, Strawberry Shortcake, and my sweet friend, Angel Cake.

Welcome to my world of sweets and sprinkles! I'm a baker and I live in Cakewalk. It's a town made out of decorated cake houses. I have a bakery right in my home!

Together we'll make lots of berrylicious crafts and recipes.

We'll have a double layer of berry good times together! My sweet pet lamb, Vanilla Icing, will join us on an adventure that's frosted with fun. So, grab your **Cake Craft Kit** and let's get started!

Angel Cake and Strawberry Shortcake's Tips for Getting Started

1. It's a berry good idea to gather everything you need before you begin a project or recipe.

2. It can be lots of fun to do these projects with a friend or favorite grown-up!

3. Whenever you see this symbol throughout the book, it means that you can find what you need in your craft kit!

4. You can find many of the materials for the projects in the book around your house. Check the grocery store, a bakery, or a craft store for supplies you don't already have.

5. Some activities in this book have this symbol. You will need a grown-up's help for the project.

Berry Funny

Q: Why did the baker throw the butter out the window?

A: She wanted to see a butter-fly!

Getting Ready to Make the Recipes

1. **Wear an apron or an old shirt to keep your clothes berry neat.**

2. **Wash your hands with soap and water. Wipe your cooking table or counter with a soapy cloth or sponge. Dry with a clean dishcloth.**

3. **Keep paper towels handy. A damp paper towel is great for wiping your hands when they get a little messy. Dry paper towels are good for cleaning up spills.**

4. **Have fun measuring, mixing, and decorating, but leave the stove stuff to a grown-up.**

Berry Funny

Q: What kind of cake always seems to make people sing?

A: A birthday cake!

Great Color Mixing

Did you know that when you mix two different shades of food coloring together, you get a whole new color? To tint your Crystal Frosting Paint in projects throughout this book, follow these combinations, using one drop of each color. You can also try coming up with your own color blends!

red + yellow = orange

yellow + green = lime

red + blue = plum

yellow + blue = green

Turn the page to frost your world with color that sparkles!

Angel Cake's Crystal Frosting Paint

Use ingredients right in your kitchen to make puffy paint that sparkles!

1. **Mix together the salt, flour, and water in a bowl. Stir until the mixture looks like thick pudding or mashed potatoes.**

What You Need

- ½ cup salt
- ½ cup flour
- ½ cup water
- Food coloring (any 2 colors)
- 2 sealable plastic freezer bags
- Kitchen scissors
- 1 sheet of construction paper (any color)
- Utensils: Measuring cups, 2 medium-sized bowls, wooden spoon

2. **Put half of the mixture into a second bowl. Stir the food coloring into the first bowl, two drops at a time, until the paint is the color you like. Repeat with the second bowl, but make the paint a different color.**

3. **Have an adult hold the two freezer bags open for you, as you spoon the mixture into each one, one color per bag.**

4. **Use scissors to snip off a teeny tiny bit of one corner on the bottom of each bag.**

5. **Use two hands to gently squeeze the bag so the paint flows out of the hole onto a piece of construction paper. Practice decorating the paper as if it were the top of a cake!**
   You'll use this paint in future projects.

Practice Decorating with Crystal Frosting Paint

Here are Angel Cake's favorite methods for decorating cakes and making great pictures with Crystal Frosting Paint:

1. **Squeeze the bag and move your hands from side to side to draw a wavy line.**

2. **Squeeze a little paint in one spot, then carefully lift the bag up as you stop squeezing to make a dot. Add more dots.**

3. **To make a flower, squeeze out a dot. Then put some dashes around it.**

Have fun! Make lots of designs! The more you design, the better you'll get!

Turn the page to make a pretty frosting picture!

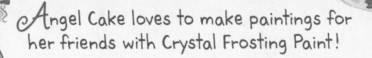

Pretty Paintings

Angel Cake loves to make paintings for her friends with Crystal Frosting Paint!

What You Need

- 1 sheet of construction paper (any color)
- Crystal Frosting Paint (2 colors in sealed bags with the corners snipped)

2. Draw a wavy line down both sides of the paper.

1. Place your sheet of paper on the table sideways. Using one color of Crystal Frosting Paint (see page 6), make a straight line across the top and bottom of the paper.

3. Draw a half-circle in the middle of the paper. This is the top of your cupcake. Draw the bottom part below it, as shown.

4. Using another color of paint, make a cherry in the middle of the top of the half-circle. Add dashes around it. Draw a few lines on the cupcake cup.

Berry Funny

Q: What kind of cake is the biggest flop?

A: An upside-down cake!

5. Draw four dots around the cupcake. Add dashes around each dot to make flowers. Place smaller dots around your cupcake for decoration. Let your designs dry overnight. Crystal Frosting Paint is berry special. You'll see it sparkle more as it dries!

Here's More: When you decorate with Crystal Frosting Paint, you can pretend that a piece of paper is the top of a large cake! Put designs around the sides, write special words on it, or draw a picture in the middle. Add flowers all over the place!

Turn the page to see how you can build and paint your own Cakewalk Castle!

Cakewalk Castle

𝓘n the village of Cakewalk where Angel Cake lives, all of the houses are tall, fancy, frosted cakes! Now you can build and decorate your own!

1. Lay a box down flat. Wrap construction paper around the top and sides of it. Tape the edges of the paper to the underside of the box. You might need to tape two pieces of paper around it, if you have a big box.

2. Repeat step 1 with your other one or two boxes.

3. Stack your wrapped boxes so the largest box is on the bottom, with the smaller boxes stacked on top. Try to stack them so that each box is set in the middle of the one below it.

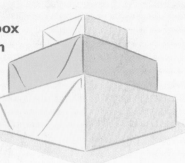

4. Take a piece of tape as long as your longest finger. Roll it inside out to make a little sticky loop. Put the tape loop under the top box so you can attach it to the one below. Make more tape loops and put them under each box so that all of the boxes are taped together.

5. You're ready to decorate your cake! Put a piece of newspaper under your stacked boxes to catch drips and spills. Use bags of Crystal Frosting Paint to add designs around each box in your Cakewalk Castle.

6. Let your Cakewalk Castle dry overnight. See the crystals sparkle when it dries!

Did you notice how your Crystal Frosting Paint sparkles?
The sparkling crystals you see are berry cool little rocks of salt!

Here's More: Your Cakewalk Castle makes a great decoration for a special birthday. You can give your Cakewalk Castle to a friend as a birthday surprise!

Turn the page to make a place to keep your sweet treats!

Sweet Treat Jar

Angel Cake loves to use this jar to store sweet treats, baking ingredients, and her favorite treasures!

What You Need

- 1 empty, clear plastic container with a lid (like a peanut butter jar, or an empty spice container)
- Waxed paper
- Scissors
- Tissue paper
- Craft paper
- Water
- Glue
- Paintbrush
- Utensils: Spoon, paper or plastic cup

1. Clean and dry the empty container. Rest it on a piece of waxed paper.

2. Use scissors to cut shapes, designs, and pictures from colorful tissue paper and craft paper. Cut the shapes so that they will fit on your container.

6. **Repeat steps 4 and 5, sticking more colorful shapes onto the container. Overlap the edges of the shapes. Cover the whole container with colorful paper. Let it dry overnight.**

3. **Put 10 spoonfuls of water into a cup. Add a spoonful of glue. Stir with the spoon until the mixture looks like milk.**

4. **Use the paintbrush to brush a little glue mix onto a spot on the side of the container.**

5. **Lay a piece of colorful paper onto the wet spot. It will stick right on. Brush over the piece of paper with more glue mix.**

Here's More: You can make big Sweet Treat Jars to hold all of your baking ingredients, like sugar, flour, and salt. Or make small containers to store cinnamon and sprinkles.

Turn the page to make a special scent to store in a Sweet Treat Jar!

Smell as Sweet as Angel Cake

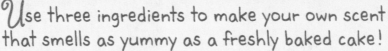

Use three ingredients to make your own scent that smells as yummy as a freshly baked cake!

What You Need

- Baby oil
- Shampoo
- Vanilla extract
- Small container with tight-fitting lid (like a small jar, bottle, or Sweet Treat Container)
- Glitter glue
- Stickers
- Utensils: Spoon

2. Add 1 or 2 big drops of vanilla to the mixture. Then stir again.

4. Rub a drop of your Angel Cake scent on your wrist! Store the rest of your special perfume in the container, with the lid on tight.

3. Decorate the container with glitter glue designs and stickers.

Here's More: Make your own scent recipes to give as gifts! Instead of vanilla, squeeze a little wedge of lemon or orange into your mixture for a fruity scent!

1. Put a spoonful of baby oil in the container and add a spoonful of shampoo. Stir until the shampoo and baby oil are mixed.

Who smells sweet and is soft and cuddly as can be? Look at the next page to see!

Angel Cake's Sweet Little Lamb, Vanilla Icing

This little lamb follows Angel Cake everywhere she goes!

What You Need

- 9-inch round paper plate
- Pipe cleaner
- White glue
- 20—40 cotton balls
- Crayons
- Paper
- Scissors
- Optional: Angel Cake perfume (see page 14)

1. Poke both ends of a pipe cleaner through the back of the plate about 1 inch from the rim. Twist two inches of the ends around each other on the front of the plate. Now you have a hanger for your plate.

2. Spread glue all over the front of the plate with your finger. Press cotton balls into the wet glue. Cover the entire plate, including the ends of the pipe cleaner. Let the glue dry.

3. Use crayons to draw eyes, ears, a nose, and a mouth on paper. Cut each one out with scissors. Glue them onto the cotton balls to make Vanilla Icing's face.

4. Dip your finger into some Smell as Sweet as Angel Cake perfume (see page 14). Dab some perfume onto the cotton to make Vanilla Icing smell sweet as can be!

Turn the page to see Angel Cake's most amazing layer cake!

Angel Cake's A-maze-ing Creation

Angel Cake has made her biggest and sweetest cake ever!

Can you make your way through the cake?
Use your finger to trace a path from the word "Start" to the word "Finish."

Start

Whip Cream

Finish

Turn the page for a fun game you can make and play with a friend!

Angel Cake's Cupcake Concentration Game

Angel Cake and I love to play this matching game together! But be careful — you might get berry hungry!

What You Need

- 1 sheet of thin white paper
- Cupcake pattern (on page 38)
- Colored pencils
- White or light-colored construction paper or card stock
- Scissors
- Glitter glue
- 2 Berry Sweet Players

Set Up

1. Place a piece of thin paper over the small cupcake pattern on page 38. Trace over the cupcake outline with a colored pencil and cut out the cupcake.

2. Trace around your cupcake stencil on construction paper or card stock. Trace as many cupcakes as you can on each piece of paper and cut them out. You'll need to make 24 cupcakes total.

3. Using your colored pencils and glitter glue, decorate the cupcakes two at a time, so that they look exactly the same. Every cupcake should have a match. You'll need 12 pairs of matching cupcakes. Here are some ideas to make each pair look different:

- Add a berry, gumdrop, or cherry to the top of your cupcake.
- Color the cupcakes with different colors.
- Decorate the frosting. Try sprinkle dots, glitter glue candy circles, or swirly designs.

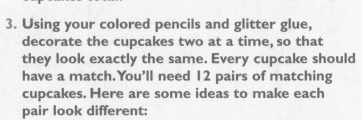

Now it's time to play
Angel Cake's Cupcake Game!

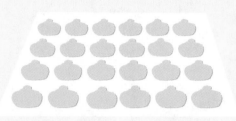

1. **Turn all your cupcake cut-outs upside down so you can't see their designs. Move them around to mix them up. Now line up the cupcakes into four rows, with six cupcakes in each row. Decide who goes first.**

It's a match!   *Try again!*

2. **Player 1 turns over two cupcakes from any row. Do the cupcakes match?**

   🧁 **If it's a match, Player 1 takes the pair and takes another turn!**

   🧁 **If it's not a match, Player 1 turns the cupcakes back over, and then it's Player 2's turn.**

Here's the trick: Remember the cupcakes you've seen until your next turn! When you turn over a cupcake, try to remember if you've seen its match before!

3. **Keep taking turns matching cupcakes. The player with the most pairs after all the cupcakes are matched—wins!**

Here's More: You can play this game by yourself, or you can play with lots of friends. Trace and cut out the cupcakes, then work together to decorate matching pairs.

Turn the page to make some pretty paper projects!

Berry Beautiful Cake Collage

This cake collage is just as sweet as Angel Cake's yummiest cake!

1. **Sketch a cake on your cardboard. Draw as many layers as you like. Once you're happy with your cake shape, cut it out.**

What You Need

- Piece of cardboard (from a recycled cereal box or a piece of poster board)
- Pencil
- Scissors
- Craft paper
- Gift wrap
- School glue or glue stick
- Ribbon
- Stickers
- Tissue paper

2. **Now cut craft paper and gift wrap into all different shapes and sizes, from as small as a strawberry to as big as a cupcake. You'll use the shapes to cover your cake.**

3. Glue the colorful pieces to your cake shape, overlapping them so that the entire cardboard shape is covered. You can cut more paper shapes if you run out.

6. Take 10–12 inches of ribbon and fold it in half. Glue the ends of the ribbon to the back of your cake to make a loop. Now you can hang your berry special cake collage on a wall or door!

4. Cut pieces of ribbon to fit across each layer of your cake and glue them on. Press stickers onto the ribbons for extra sparkle!

5. Crumple up some of your tiny sheets of tissue paper to make small flowers. Glue them across the top of each layer of your cake for decoration.

Here's More: Share a birthday surprise with this beautiful decoration! Hang it on a friend's door or give it as a gift.

Turn the page to make a bunch of sweet paper flowers !

Angel Cake's Pretty Paper Flowers

These pretty flowers bloom more and more with each step!

2. **Fold the rectangle in half, bringing the short sides together to make a smaller square.**

3. **Find the corner on the square that has no folds. Cut a curve around this corner.**

What You Need

🍓 Construction paper or card stock in different colors

🍓 Ruler

🍓 Scissors

🍓 Glue

🍓 Stickers

1. **Cut a 4-x-4-inch square out of a sheet of paper. Fold the paper square in half to make a rectangle.**

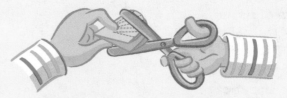

4. **Keeping the paper folded, cut away some skinny triangles from the curve you just made. This will make flower petal shapes.**

5. Unfold the paper to see your flower.

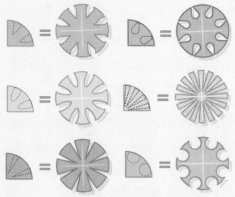

6. If you want different flower petals, cut along the red dotted lines shown above for different shapes.

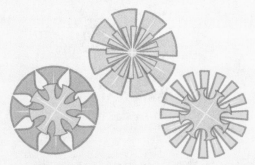

7. To make fun little petals for the middle of your flower, cut another 2-x-2-inch paper square. Repeat steps 2 through 5. Glue the petals onto your flower.

8. To make the center circle for your flower, cut a 1-x-1-inch square. Repeat steps 2 and 3, and glue the circle on top of your flower. Press some stickers on for sparkle! You can cut a leaf out of a green sheet of paper and glue it to the back of your flower, if you like.

Here's More: Here are some ways to use your Pretty Paper Flowers:
- Decorate a straw hat
- Decorate Vanilla Icing's woolly coat (on page 15)
- Decorate a card

Turn the page for some yummilicious treats!

Angel Cake's Easy-to-Bake Cupcakes

These cupcakes are Angel Cake's favorite snack to share with her berry best friends!

What You Need

- 1 stick of butter
- 1 cup sugar
- 2 eggs
- 2 teaspoons vanilla extract
- 1 ½ cups flour
- 2 teaspoons baking powder
- ½ cup milk
- Utensils: Cupcake pan, paper cupcake liners, saucepan, 2 large mixing bowls, measuring cups and spoons, 2 wooden spoons

Makes: 12-15 yummy cupcakes

1. An adult should preheat the oven to 350°F. Put the paper cupcake liners in the cupcake pan.

2. Have an adult melt butter in a small saucepan over low heat. Once it's melted, pour the butter into a mixing bowl, and add the sugar. Stir well.

3. **Crack open and add the eggs. Stir with a spoon for one minute. Then add in the vanilla until it blends in with the yellow batter.**

6. **Spoon the cupcake batter into each paper-lined cup of the cupcake pan so that each cup is ²/₃ full.**

4. **In another bowl, mix the flour and baking powder. Then add the mix to the first bowl with the yellow batter.**

7. **Bake your cupcakes in the oven for 20 to 25 minutes, until the cupcakes are golden yellow, like the color of Angel Cake's hair. An adult should remove the cupcake pan from the oven. Let the cupcakes cool completely before decorating them.**

Angel Cake's Baking Tip:
You know your cupcakes are baked just right when they spring back up when you gently press down on the top of them with the tip of your finger!

5. **Add the milk and stir.**

Turn the page to frost your cupcakes in bright colors!

Fun Flavored Frosting

What makes Angel Cake's frosting so berrylicious? It takes only four ingredients.

1. **With an adult's help, combine the powdered sugar, butter, and milk in a large bowl with a mixer. Mix until the frosting is smooth and all of the ingredients are blended together.**

What You Need

- 2 cups powdered sugar
- ½ stick of butter
- 2 tablespoons milk
- Powdered drink mix, in flavors like fruit punch, orange, lemonade, blueberry, grape, or lime-ade (each flavor will make a special frosting with a different color, scent, and taste)
- Utensils: 1 large bowl, 2 or 3 small bowls, mixer, spoon, butter knife

    Makes: About 1 cup of sweet frosting

2. **To make flavored frosting, spoon ½ cup of frosting into a small bowl. Add a pinch of flavored drink mix. Stir until the drink mix is well-blended into the icing. Keep adding the drink mix, a little at a time, and stirring until the frosting tastes the way you like it. You can make different flavors in several small bowls.**

3. To frost your cupcakes, spread a spoonful of frosting on the top of each cupcake with a butter knife.

Delightful Decorating

After you've baked your cupcakes, gather up special sweets! Create your own designs by sprinkling or gently pressing the decorations into the icing. Here are some ideas:

sprinkles

colored sugar

jelly beans

candy confetti

berries

licorice bits

gumdrops

mini marshmallows

Turn the page to make your cupcakes special and sweet, just like you!

Angel Cake's Yummylicious Cupcake Combinations

Pick a yummy cupcake flavor and add a special frosting for a treat that is as sweet as can be!

Bake a Luscious Cupcake!

It's so easy! Just start with the cupcake recipe on pages 24–25 and add one special step (after step 5), just before you spoon the batter into the cupcake pan.

Real Raspberry Cupcakes

Stir one cup of raspberry preserves into the cupcake batter. Spoon 3 or 4 tablespoons of batter into cupcake cups in the pan, and bake as directed.

Strawberry Swirl Cupcakes

(This is Strawberry Shortcake's favorite cupcake!)

Stir one cup of strawberry preserves into the cupcake batter. Spoon 3 or 4 tablespoons of batter into cupcake cups in the pan, and bake as directed.

Tangy Lemon Cupcakes

Cut two lemons in half with a butter knife and squeeze the juice from the halves into the batter. Spoon 3 or 4 tablespoons of batter into cupcake cups in the pan, and bake as directed.

Chocolate Fudge Cupcakes

Mix ¼ cup cocoa with the cupcake batter. Spoon 3 or 4 tablespoons of batter into cupcake cups in the pan, and bake as directed.

Mix up a Flav-orite Frosting!

It's a snap! Just put all of the ingredients in a bowl and blend with an electric mixer.

Strawberry Frosting

- 🍓 1 stick (½ cup) butter
- 🍓 2 cups powdered sugar
- 🍓 1 fresh strawberry, cut into small pieces

Peanut Butter Frosting

- 🍓 2 cups powdered sugar
- 🍓 ½ cup peanut butter
- 🍓 ¼ cup milk
- 🍓 1½ teaspoons vanilla extract

Whipped Cream Frosting

- 🍓 2 cups whipping cream or heavy cream
- 🍓 ¼ cup powdered sugar
- 🍓 ½ teaspoon vanilla extract

Chocolate Frosting

- 🍓 2 cups powdered sugar
- 🍓 3 tablespoons cocoa
- 🍓 1 stick (½ cup) butter (softened)
- 🍓 2 tablespoons milk

Which frosting will you add to your cupcakes?

Turn the page to make a treat that's full of surprises!

Angel Cake Surprise

*A*ngel Cake and I love to make this treat with berries from my strawberry patch and freshly baked cake from her bakery!

What You Need

- 2 cups cold milk
- 1 box instant vanilla pudding (4 serving size)
- 1 angel cake or pound cake
- 1 cup orange juice
- Fruit: 2 bananas (sliced), 1 cup strawberries (sliced), and 1 cup blueberries
- Optional: Whipped topping or shredded coconut
- Utensils: Measuring cups, mixing bowl, whisk, spoons, clear plastic or glass cups or bowls

Makes: Six sweet servings

1. **Pour milk in a mixing bowl. Stir in the instant pudding mix with a whisk. Keep stirring for 2 minutes to make pudding.**

2. **Tear small chunks from your angel cake or pound cake and drop them in the bottom of a clear bowl or cup. Arrange them so that they cover the bottom of the bowl.**

3. Sprinkle a little orange juice over the angel cake chunks in the bowl with a spoon, so that the cake pieces are moist. Then, spoon enough pudding into the bowl to cover the cake chunks.

4. Add a few banana and strawberry slices, and blueberries over the pudding in each bowl. The cake, pudding, and fruit make one complete layer of your Angel Cake Surprise.

5. Repeat steps 2 through 5 twice to make two more layers.

6. Once you've made three layers, you can top your Angel Cake Surprise with some whipped topping, or you can sprinkle some shredded coconut on top. Eat your sweet surprise with a spoon!

Use a clear bowl to make your Angel Cake Surprise so that you can see the layers of fruit and yummy-ness as you build the treat.
If you use a regular bowl, it will taste just as delicious!

Here's More: Invite your friends over to make this sweet treat with you! Ask each friend to bring her favorite fruit to add to the recipe—you'll be surprised how berry good it tastes!

Turn the page to make a crispy, crunchy cupcake treat!

Crunchy Crispy Cakes

Angel Cake loves to make these tasty treats. They are shaped like her favorite snack—cupcakes!

What You Need

- Cooking spray
- 4 cups regular marshmallows (about a 10 oz. package)
- 3 tablespoons butter or margarine
- 6 cups crispy rice cereal
- Small, colorful candies
- Utensils: Large mixing bowl, 24-cup mini-muffin pan or 12-cup regular-size muffin pan, saucepan, big spoon, butter knife, cup

  Makes: About 18 crunchy and crispy treats

1. **Coat a large mixing bowl and muffin pan with cooking spray. Set it aside.**

2. **Have an adult melt the marshmallows and butter in a saucepan over low heat, stirring until the mixture is smooth.**

3. With an adult's help, pour the marshmallow mixture into the large mixing bowl you coated with spray in step 1. Add the crispy rice cereal to the bowl, and stir until all the cereal is coated with the melted marshmallow. The mixture will be very sticky!

4. Have an adult help you spoon the cereal and marshmallow mixture into the muffin cups.

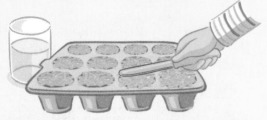

5. Dip a butter knife into some water so that it's wet. Use the butter knife to press the cereal and marshmallow mixture into the cups of the muffin pan. Wet the butter knife again, if it starts to get sticky.

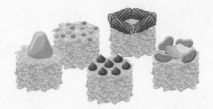

6. Press colorful candies into the tops of your Crunchy Crispy Cakes to decorate them. Let them set for about 30 minutes. Then pop them out of the pan. Yummy!

Here's More: You can use your favorite little candies to decorate your Crunchy Crispy Cakes. Here are some sweet suggestions:
* Chocolate chips
* Colorful, candy-coated chocolate candies
* Small bits of red licorice
* Jellybeans

Turn the page to make a berry special cupcake book!

The Berry Best Cupcake Recipe Book

Angel Cake keeps all her favorite cupcake recipes in this berry pretty book!

What You Need

- 1 sheet of thin paper
- Cupcake pattern (on page 38)
- Markers (any colors)
- Scissors
- 3 sheets of white or light-colored paper
- Glue
- Glitter glue

2. Trace around your stencil on your paper. Draw 6 large cupcakes and cut them out. These will be your recipe book pages.

1. To make your cupcake stencil, place a piece of thin paper over the cupcake pattern on page 38. Trace over the outline of the large cupcake with the cherry on top using a marker. Then cut it out.

3. Use markers and glitter glue to decorate one large cupcake as the cover of your recipe book.

"Choco-nut
Cupcake Recipe"
Chocolate Cupcake
Peanut Butter Frosting
One Gumdrop

4. **To make your own cupcake recipe, choose a cupcake flavor, a frosting flavor, and a special decoration. Make up a fun name for your combination, and write the recipe on one large cupcake shape. Decorate the page with your markers. You can fit five recipes in your book (if you are using 6 cupcakes).**

"Yummylicious
Cupcake Recipe"
Strawberry Cupcake
Whipped Cream Frosting
One Strawberry

5. **To make your book, put your cupcake pages together, with the cover on top. On the cupcake cover, put a little glue on the back of the cherry. Press the cover onto the front of the first page's cherry, so they stick together. Keep putting glue on the back of each page's cherry and sticking it onto the front of the next page until all the pages are glued together. Let dry.**

Cupcake Combinations

Mix and match cupcakes with fun frosting flavors and berry special toppings to create your own recipes! Make up names for your sweet cupcake treats!

 Pick a cupcake flavor!
vanilla, real raspberry, chocolate fudge, tangy lemon, strawberry swirl

 Pick a frosting flavor!
chocolate, peanut butter, strawberry, whipped cream

 Pick a special topping!
gumdrops, mini marshmallows, chocolate chips, sprinkles, gummy bears, colored sugar, crushed nuts

My Berry Best Cupcake Recipes!

Here's one of Angel Cake's favorite combinations:
chocolate fudge cupcakes
peanut-butter frosting
mini marshmallows

Turn the page to make a cupcake that really pops!

Angel Cake's Pop-Up Cupcake Card

Angel Cake loves to make these cards when she invites her friends over for a cupcake party!

What You Need

* 2 sheets of construction paper (any color)
* Crayons
* 1 sheet of thin paper
* Cupcake pattern (on page 38)
* Pencil
* Scissors
* Glitter glue
* Tape

2. Place a piece of thin paper over the large cupcake pattern on page 38 and trace over the outline with a pencil. Cut out the cupcake. This will be your pattern.

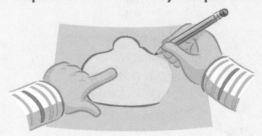

1. To make the card, fold a piece of construction paper in half. Use crayons to decorate the front of the card.

3. Place the cupcake pattern onto another piece of construction paper. Use a pencil to trace around it. Set the pattern aside. Cut out the cupcake with scissors. Decorate your cupcake with crayons and glitter glue!

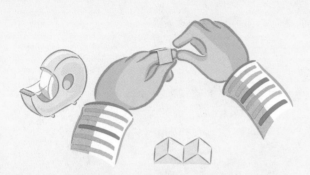

4. To make your cupcake pop-out, draw two 2-x-1-inch rectangles on construction paper. Fold each rectangle in half, then in half again. Open the folds. Wrap one rectangle around your finger to make a rectangular block with open ends. Tape the edges together and take it off your finger. Repeat with the other rectangle, so you have two blocks.

6. Attach the cupcake to the center of the inside of the card, so that the fold in the cupcake lines up with the fold of the card. (One paper block should be taped on each side of the card's fold.) Slowly close the card so the paper blocks flatten. Open the card to see your cupcake pop out!

5. Fold the cupcake in half with the design inside. Tape the paper blocks to the back of the cupcake, one on each side of the fold.

Here's More: Write a berry special message inside your card to tell a friend, "You are as sweet as can be!"

Angel Cake's Answer Page

Angel Cake's A-maze-ing Creation
(pages 16–17)

Large Cupcake Pattern
(pages 34–37)

Small Cupcake Pattern
(pages 18–19)

More Sweet Strawberryland Adventures COMING SOON!

To Our Berry Sweet Friend,
    We hope you had a sweet time visiting Cakewalk and making all the projects in this frosting-filled adventure! Come back for more delicious Strawberryland fun soon!

Your berry best friends,
Strawberry Shortcake,
ANGEL CAKE, and Vanilla Icing